COLUMBIA ESSAYS ON MODERN WRITERS

NUMBER 11 · PRICE $.65

ALAIN ROBBE-GRILLET

by Bruce Morrissette

Alain Robbe-Grillet

by BRUCE MORRISSETTE

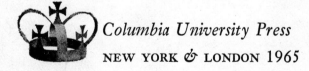

Columbia University Press

NEW YORK & LONDON 1965

COLUMBIA ESSAYS ON MODERN WRITERS is a series of critical studies of English, Continental, and other writers whose works are of contemporary artistic and intellectual significance.

Editor: William York Tindall

Advisory Editors

Jacques Barzun   W.T.H. Jackson   Joseph A. Mazzeo   Justin O'Brien

Alain Robbe-Grillet is Number 11 in the series.

BRUCE MORRISSETTE is Professor of French Literature at the University of Chicago. He is the author of a number of books on French literature, including *The Life and Works of Mademoiselle Desjardins* and *The Great Rimbaud Forgery.*

Alain Robbe-Grillet

Alain Robbe-Grillet's biographer might point out that, like every artist, he has taken materials from his own life. But can biography explain how these materials are transformed into novels and films? The young Robbe-Grillet's fascination with the lichens and rock plants of his native Breton seacoast (he was born in 1922, at Brest, of parents who had migrated there from the Jura) bore results not in the career of agronomic engineer for which his technical training prepared him, but rather in the habits of observation of microstructures and their scientifically phrased descriptions which lie, at least partly, at the source of his so-called objectal prose vocabulary of surface geometries. A biographer would recognize in the cliffs and sea gulls of *The Voyeur* those of Ouessant or the Finistère, and in the plantation house and banana trees of *Jealousy* the verandas and fronds of Martinique, where the author worked as an overseer. But these are only points of departure, like the cities of the Low Countries found in *The Erasers* and *In the Labyrinth*, the baroque châteaux visited in Bavaria that became the setting of *Last Year at Marienbad*, or the bazaars and mosques of Istanbul filmed in *L'Immortelle*.

Where a more conventional author would seek to communicate the "real" flavor of a setting, exotic or familiar, Robbe-Grillet superimposes a grill that converts any locale into a portion of his personal universe. A distinct aesthetic distance separates the real world from the world of Robbe-Grillet's novels and films. When this re-created world is subjected to distortion through the vision of a tormented protagonist, it

[3]

undergoes further radical change. No biographical approach could account fully for most aspects of his writings, and it would be vain to seek more facts. Of what literary importance is it, for example, to know that he worked as a deported laborer in a German tank factory during World War II? At most, one learns from such investigations the external fact that it was in the environs of this factory at Nuremberg that he met Claude Ollier, with whom he engaged in literary discussions that doubtless figured in his later decision (taken while hospitalized in Martinique) to abandon agronomy for a writer's career.

This career, certainly one of the most brilliant in contemporary French literature, began with *The Erasers* (*Les Gommes*) in 1953. Robbe-Grillet had already written *Un Régicide*, most of which is still unpublished. Closeted in the eighth-floor walk-up *chambre de bonne* which he occupied in the Rue Gassendi, he wrote *The Voyeur*, which won him the Prix des Critiques in 1955 and launched his present vogue. Robbe-Grillet now turns out his novels, essays, and scenarios at an apartment near the Bois de Boulogne in Paris and at the small, elegant Louis XIV château of Le Mesnil-au-Grain where he lives with his wife, Catherine, commuting when necessary from nearby Caen to Paris for short stays and to pursue his editorial duties at the Éditions de Minuit, where he has been Jérôme Lindon's literary director since 1955. This press, which is the acknowledged center of the *nouveau roman* group, has published not only Robbe-Grillet's works, but also those of Samuel Beckett, Claude Simon, Michel Butor, Marguerite Duras, Robert Pinget, Claude Ollier, Jean Ricardou, and Nathalie Sarraute. In a sense, the whole idea of a "New Novel," however vague the designation may be, is the creation of Robbe-Grillet and Lindon. Aside from all considerations of the critical validity of the term, it has served the above-mentioned authors well and publicized their existence around the world.

[4]

Robbe-Grillet's entire creative work, as in the case of a Picasso or a Stravinsky, may be seen as a basic unity evolving through distinct stylistic phases. "Stylistic" is used here, of course, not in the rhetorical sense, but in the sense of organized forms.

For, the idea that *form* is essential to the novel is a fundamental tenet of Robbe-Grillet. "What is important for me in the novel," he remarked to me recently, "is *structure*, or form. This is why I appreciate a 'bad' novel like *The Postman Always Rings Twice*. It is *structured*. The accident happens twice, in the same way but with different results." One could point out that in his own novels, Robbe-Grillet has employed the doubling of events in circular structures not dissimilar to that of Cain's *Postman:* the two "identical" murders of *The Erasers,* the apparent repetition of events in *Last Year at Marienbad,* even two "identical" automobile accidents, as in Cain's novel, in the film *L'Immortelle.* But form in Robbe-Grillet is a far more complicated matter than mere over-all or general patterns. Form for him involves serial arrangements of objects having specific designs (figures-of-eight, *V*'s, *Y*'s, and other patterns), interior duplications of themes and characters, restructured chronology, and many more devices that will be examined later. What is important is that to Robbe-Grillet, a literary work can only acquire its meaning, and hence its value, through form.

One may use other means of access, besides form, to the sometimes difficult works of Robbe-Grillet, but it is to form that one must return in the end. Among other paths of investigation (after eliminating that of biography) are the ideas he has expressed in his various "manifestoes," concerning the obsolescence of psychological analysis of characters, the refusal of ideological interpretations or justifications of the novel (including a rejection of Sartrian "engagement" in a political

[5]

sense), the essential subjectivity of "objects" in the novel, and the like. That these ideas bear some relation to his works is evident; but to engage in critical effort aimed solely at establishing agreement or disagreement between these "theories" and the works themselves seems a sterile task. Similarly, identification of purely literary influences or "sources," while it may lead to clarification of certain points, has more scholarly than aesthetic importance. Robbe-Grillet has often spoken of his interest in Joyce, Faulkner, Kafka, Raymond Roussel, and lesser writers like Graham Greene, Simenon, and James M. Cain. It is often possible to show such influences at work, as examples will later illustrate.

It is also possible to point out certain obviously *pathological* aspects of Robbe-Grillet's fiction. These have led some critics, like Otto Hahn, to attempt to psychoanalyze the author: the sadism of *The Voyeur*, the paranoia of *Jealousy*, the hyper-suggestibility and *folie à deux* of *Marienbad* become a pretext for engaging in speculations concerning Robbe-Grillet's attitude toward his mother and other aspects of his psyche. Robbe-Grillet is, of course, quite aware of the pathological elements in his work. "I feel like the most normal of men," he said one evening in Paris, "yet most of my main characters are mad." Traces of early poring over manuals of psychopathology (like that of Stekel) may be found throughout his novels, as in the famous passage of the counting of banana trees in *Jealousy* (a Stekelian symptom related to psychic impotence and masturbation). Bernard Pingaud has pointed out that hyper-attentive descriptions, similar to those of Robbe-Grillet, are found in the notebooks of paranoiacs. But here again, as in the case of materials furnished by travel, identification of the "source" discloses no more than a point of departure, which however anecdotal, picturesque, or curious in itself, fails to explain the ultimate meaning of the fiction in which it appears.

[6]

Yet it would be foolish to deny the presence of these elements, or to refuse to accord to them their proper place in understanding Robbe-Grillet's works. Much of the confusion among his readers and critics may be attributed to the shortcomings of an excessively single-intentioned approach. For example, the first influential critic of Robbe-Grillet, Roland Barthes, was almost able to persuade readers that the main, if not the only, importance of Robbe-Grillet's work was its use of descriptions of *things*. To Barthes, Robbe-Grillet was a *chosiste*. His plots, if any, were only a pretext, or, as in *The Erasers*, an ironic parody of myth, serving as an excuse for including "Einsteinian" descriptions of objects whose function was to deny all metaphysical implications, to present a world of neutral "surfaces" devoid of depth in a universe of characters without psychology or interiority of any kind. Barthes was, in fact, using Robbe-Grillet's descriptive techniques to buttress his own attack on all forms of contemporary religious or moral humanism, especially the "humanistic" metaphysics of a Camus or of those who in Barthes's view were seeking to "recuperate" atheistic or agnostic man by bringing him into an emotionalized theological system of "tragic" separation from Nature, or God. Such ideas attracted Robbe-Grillet himself, who made use of similar arguments in his essay "Nature, Humanisme, Tragédie" (translated as "Old 'Values' and the New Novel").

A number of critics, following Barthes's lead, took the position that any discussion of the "plot" of a Robbe-Grillet novel was a sort of heresy, especially if the attempt involved even a provisional "reconstruction" of linear chronology (in *Jealousy*, for example), or the establishment of a hypothesis in order to interpret elliptical omissions (as with the implied guilt of Mathias, protagonist of *The Voyeur*, whose sadistic crime a number of critics sought to dismiss). This *noli me tangere* attitude toward Robbe-Grillet's plot constructions is still prevalent among the so-called *Tel Quel* group of his critics, including writers like Gérard Genette and Hélène Prigogine. It is perhaps not an exaggeration to say, however, that the *Tel Quel* group, with its ambiguous terminology and absence of clear ideas, functions more as a ceremonial cult than as a productive critical enterprise, and that the image of Robbe-Grillet's works that it seeks to foster remains imprecise, if not seriously deformed.

Other evidence shows to what an extent differences of opinion divide critics of Robbe-Grillet today. When my study of his novels (*Les Romans de Robbe-Grillet*) appeared in 1963, it was prefaced with an essay by Roland Barthes which struck a number of reviewers as something of an oddity in that it took an almost diametrically opposite point of view from that of the book itself. To Barthes, my attempt to develop a rounded picture of Robbe-Grillet's work, neglecting nothing (including plot and implied psychology) that it seemed to contain, appeared as another act of "recuperation" by imperialistic humanism of an author who had tried to escape its grasp. As Barthes phrased it, "Between the two Robbe-Grillets, the Robbe-Grillet No. 1, *chosiste,* and the Robbe-Grillet No. 2, 'humanist,' between the Robbe-Grillet of the early criticism [that is, of Barthes himself] and the Robbe-Grillet of Bruce Morrissette, must one choose?" Since the answer seemed to be Yes, the remainder of Barthes's preface was given over to expressions of regret at seeing the old "non-significant" Robbe-Grillet of the "mat surfaces" threatened with replacement by a Robbe-Grillet who creates levels of meaning, devises plots, uses psychology (if not psychological analysis), employs things or objects not in neutral isolation or detachment but in a referential manner—as objective correlatives or supports of human emotions: in a word, by a Robbe-Grillet who, for all the newness of his techniques, composes *novels.* Readers must decide for themselves whether the discovery of polyvalent implications and meanings in Robbe-Grillet distorts his aesthetic purposes. If the conception of a Robbe-Grillet intent only on microscopic descriptions of *things* is inadequate to explain his complicated art, what are the principles that underlie these novels and films with their new modes and structures?

In his earliest prose texts, such as the one-page pieces "Molds" (*Moisissures*) and "The Guardian Angel" (*L'Ange gardien*), which have never been published, the two basic aspects of Robbe-Grillet are already revealed: his preoccupation with minute description in the first, and with psychosadism in the second. "Molds" contains the kind of *chosiste* depiction that Barthes especially esteems: microscopic details of colored spots and bands of mildew in laboratory bottles, a mass of velvet pustules exhaling a foul odor. One is reminded of Jean-Paul Sartre's viscous and putrefied objects in *Nausea*, certainly one of Robbe-Grillet's immediate stylistic sources. But there is already the geometric and mathematical precision, the close neutral scrutiny, and much of the characteristic vocabulary, of his later descriptive passages. "The Guardian Angel" is an almost descriptionless account, largely in dialogue, of the murder of a young girl stabbed by a passing stranger. It is close enough to the "suppressed" crime of the hero of *The Voyeur* to be thought of almost as the "missing page" of that novel, and illustrates the early presence of this persistent psychopathological theme in Robbe-Grillet.

Other short pieces written and published from 1954 to 1962, and now collected in *Instantanés* (1962), illustrate original formal techniques. A number of these "Snapshots" have appeared in English. In "Three Reflected Visions" we find two relatively impersonal descriptions and one brief narrative episode. Of the former, "The Dressmaker's Dummy" may be considered an experiment in the suppressed first-person or *je-néant* mode later to be used in *Jealousy*: the point of view, with its rotations, emerges from a consciousness inside the text which the reader must assume, thus placing himself at the observational center. The panoramic turning of the text (about the mannequin and room) will be repeated in *The Voyeur* and *Jealousy*, as well as in Robbe-Grillet's films. While a mirror provides the "reflection" in "The Dummy," it is, in "The Wrong Direction," a pool of rain water that, as in some seventeenth-century baroque poems, reflects an "inverted world." A man comes to the edge of this pool, and after a moment of hesitation reminiscent of Frost's famous poem of the pause by snowy woods, turns and goes back the way he came. The theme of mistaken direction is used again in "The Way Back." Some boys hiking across an inlet complete the circle of an island, lose their way, are trapped by high water, and are rowed away by a deaf fisherman who seems intent to set forth into the raging sea. The seacoast again provides the scene for "The Shore," a hauntingly beautiful piece describing the progress of three children along a beach beneath high cliffs, the tracks they leave in the sand, and the cyclic paths of sea birds that come in, land, fly out, and return further on, while at each point an identical small wave breaks "with a rustling noise of gravel rolling."

In an interior, more artificial setting, "Scene" depicts an actor with the back of his head to the audience, seated before a pile of dictionaries on a desk. As he writes, a violent knocking occurs at the door of his heavily curtained room. He waits; the knocks grow less insistent; steps are heard retreating down a long corridor. On a cigarette butt traces of lipstick can be seen. To this point, the text is written so that no reference to sex is made (*i.e.*, no "he" or other word revealing gender), but now the audience can see (although still from behind) that it is a man. Obeying disembodied commands from an offstage director, he returns to his desk and resumes writing. Elements of this "scene" will recur in the treatment of the "narrator's" room of *In the Labyrinth;* its resemblance to scenes in Ionesco, Adamov, or Beckett suggests a *rapport* with the "theatre of the absurd."

"In the Corridors of the Métro" is a three-part study of the movements of crowds and individuals up and down the escalators of a subway station, with the countermovements of staring, fixed eyes, and a number of carefully described types of persons, with their specific clothing and accessories. The displacement of "rigid groups" whose heads suddenly turn in a chain reaction when the topmost person looks back; the movement of the crowd along corridors posted with series of the same advertisement; the crowd stopped in front of the automatic door that closes on the approach of a train, allowing them to look upward toward the platform, where they can see only the immobile shoes and socks of men waiting to board the train—all these aspects of Paris *métro* maneuvers are noted and arranged with great formal skill.

Latest of Robbe-Grillet's short texts is the *fin-de-siècle* sketch "The Secret Room," dedicated to the decadent late nineteenth-century painter Gustave Moreau, whose over-wrought canvases were popular among the surrealists and who influenced painters like Max Ernst. The secret room is an underground, vaulted dungeon where a nude girl lies slain, sacrificed or executed while her arms and legs are held spread out by rings embedded in the stone floor. Cushions, velvet tapestries, and varicolored rugs adorn this Oriental prison. Perfume is burning in a metal stand. A man in a long cloak strides up a stone stairway toward the exit. But as the description of the female body continues, time moves backward and the man

[11]

is now leaning over the living victim in the moments of her death struggle, as the dagger is plunged into her bare breast, causing the trickle of blood to stream down along the course already minutely described. As a tour de force, or as a pastiche of Moreau's gory style, "The Secret Room" is a remarkable, if questionable, performance. As a reflection of certain systematic obsessions in Robbe-Grillet, the piece may have a deep psychological meaning. While going far beyond anything in his novels or films, it nevertheless fits into the sado-erotic patterns of Mathias' implied crime in *The Voyeur* and perhaps the kind of chained death that the narrator of the film *L'Immortelle* may fear for his mistress at the hands of her Turkish master.

The exact place of these short texts in the over-all study of Robbe-Grillet's works remains to be determined. Critics have, in general, accorded them little attention or importance. It would seem undeniable, however, that as samples of both writing techniques and thematic obsessions, they will prove to be a rich source of material.

Robbe-Grillet's first published novel, *The Erasers* (*Les Gommes*, 1953), contains a considerable number of the themes, forms, and techniques of his later works. If the plot is intricate and the point of view distributed among several characters, if many scenes are developed in a manner reminiscent of Simenon's Maigret novels, if there is a carefully worked out Joycean correspondence between classical myth and contemporary story, if other distinct differences separate *The Erasers* from the later novels, this prototype of the Robbe-Grilletian "*livre à venir*" is nevertheless already marked by such typical characteristics as circular structure, use of nonlinear chronology, "false" or imagined scenes, interior duplications of characters and events, concealed correspondences, serial objects, *chosiste* descriptions, "troubling" or neosymbolic objects (such as the eraser that the protagonist vainly seeks throughout the novel), metamorphoses (such as descriptions in which a drawing becomes a photograph), psychopathology, a labyrinthine, almost surrealist décor, repetitions, "frozen" scenes, echoes, verbal enigmas, and mythic allusions. All these are incorporated in a plot which, through the use of ellipse and implication, remains open-ended and ambiguous.

One may suspect that when Robbe-Grillet in later years termed the plot of *The Erasers* "purely conventional . . . and without importance to me," he was motivated by some embarrassment at the recollection of the almost excessive ingenuity with which he had transposed the myth of Oedipus into the framework of a modern detective story. Nothing "without importance" could conceivably have been so carefully constructed; besides, despite some of his claims to the contrary, Robbe-Grillet has always shown concern for story line, even if the story, as is usually the case, has a number of possible interpretations or contains apparent contradictions. In *The Erasers* there is no mention of Oedipus, but everything, from the Sophoclean motto ("Time, which watches everything, has provided the solution in spite of you") through the prologue, five "acts" (chapters), to the epilogue, relates to the "other ancient story" which in its turn may be viewed as a folkloristic transformation of a sun myth. There is no reason to suppose that Robbe-Grillet in 1953 attributed less importance to this parallelism than did Joyce to that of *Ulysses*, even though the title (*Les Gommes*) may seem to "erase" any obvious link.

Read at the level of detective story, *The Erasers* almost satisfies the criteria of the genre. In an Amsterdam-like city of canals, circular boulevards, bridges, and identical houses, Professor Dupont has apparently been assassinated by a secret group devoted to the systematic elimination of certain political figures. Central Intelligence has sent a special agent, Wallas, to investigate. Within the space of twenty-four hours (the classical unity of time), Wallas pursues a number of misleading clues (including many that seem to point to him), attempts to decipher the riddle a drunkard recites with confusing variations, decides that the murderer will return to the scene of his crime, and goes there to meet him. Dupont himself, who is not dead but in hiding, returns to his study. Wallas, believing him to be the criminal, fires, killing the man whose "murder" he had been sent to investigate, and who, from many indications in the text, may also be his father. Thus Wallas, walking, as it were, backward in time, commits at the end of his search the same murder that Oedipus had committed before undertaking his. Unaware of the inverted and hidden relationships that tie his actions to the past legend, Wallas has relived an archetypal myth.

A wealth of details and specific allusions reinforce, beneath the surface, the Oedipal framework of *The Erasers*. There is an elaborate development of the riddle of the Sphinx, including the variant "blind in the morning, incestuous at noon, and parricide in the evening," which seems especially appropriate to Wallas' case, since he is blind to his situation, is attracted erotically to his (step) mother, and kills his presumed father. The Sphinx itself appears in the changing forms assumed by debris floating in a canal ("a fabulous animal . . . with a lion's body and its great tail, and eagle's wings . . ."). Wallas notes a theme repeated on the embroidered curtains of house after house: two shepherds in antique costume giving milk to a small nude infant. Place names from the Oedipus legend—like the Rue de Corinthe and Daulis—are scattered here and there: "Daulis" is transformed into the name of the sculptor of a large marble group in a central square representing a Greek chariot like that of Laius in the classical incident of his murder by Oedipus. A post office is described in terms suitable for the oracular temple of Apollo; and the Delphic god of prophecies appears in a group of statuettes. An elaborate discussion occurs as to the meaning of the word "oblique" (Apollo *loxias*). Fully developed images of Thebes appear, in which the temples and ruins of the ancient city are fused with the villa of the "crime" and the modern city where it is committed. Wallas, who struggles to recall why his mother had brought him to this place as a child (to see a "relative"), has unresolved fantasies of playing the central role in an ancient drama enacted on temple steps. Even the particular kind of *gomme*, or gum eraser, which he tries to find, he can identify only as having a name of six letters, with the two central letters forming the syllable "di" (in French, *Oe-di-pe*). Near the end of the story, still unconscious of his Oedipal identity, Wallas notes that he has "swollen feet" from too much walking. In this fascination with hidden relationships, Robbe-Grillet even incorporated into the novel a passage involving a stairway whose twenty-two steps correspond to the major cards of the Tarot pack, as if to relate these medieval "prophetic" devices to the system of premonitions, oracles, and enigmas of the Oedipus myth.

As pervasive and obviously significant as the Oedipus parallel thus appears, the title of the novel is not *Oedipe*, but *Les Gommes*. The novel's gum eraser manifests the preoccupation, or obsession, with objects that leads to Robbe-Grillet's being termed a *chosiste*. *The Erasers* contains an additional dozen or more apparently "pure" descriptions, which were seized upon as illustrating the presence of antimetaphysical, nonsymbolical, nonreferential *choses*, things or objects whose neutral, stubborn, indifferent *être-là* ("being there") set them apart from man, gave them in their arbitrariness and contingency a sort of defiance, a refusal to be appropriated by man into his human, or humanistic, thought patterns. It should be recalled again that Sartre's novel *Nausea* made a similar use of object descriptions. Roquentin's depiction of a chestnut-tree root was also an object lesson in the "*être-là* des choses." But where Sartre freely employs metaphor and draws intellectual conclusions, Robbe-Grillet rigorously restricts himself to the external object. A famous example is the description of the section of tomato that Wallas finds on his plate in an automat:

> A quarter section of tomato quite perfect and without defect, sliced by machine from an absolutely symmetrical fruit.
> The peripheral flesh, compact and homogeneous, of a fine chemical redness, is uniformly thick between a band of shiny skin and the semicircular area where the seeds are arranged, yellow, of uniform caliber, held in place by a thin layer of greenish jelly lying alongside the swelling at the heart. The latter, of a diluted and slightly granular pink, begins, near the lower hollow, in a network of white veins, one of which stretches out towards the seeds, in a somewhat uncertain manner.
> At the top, a scarcely visible accident has occurred: a corner of the skin, detached from the flesh over the space of one or two millimeters, sticks up imperceptibly.

Despite the apparent total objectivity of this description, it is possible to find in it motifs related to the over-all meaning or content of the novel, especially the theme of uncertainty and accident in an otherwise mechanically perfect design, a notion basic to the conception of *The Erasers* and brought out in many other passages.

The *gomme*, or gum eraser, of the title is so obviously charged with erotic significance that even Roland Barthes called it a "psychiatric object," though, he adds, "the only one in the work." Each time Wallas tries to find this "soft, light, friable" eraser, which pressure instead of "deforming, reduces to dust . . . which breaks open easily in a brilliant, smooth cut, like a pearl shell," he is seized with powerful erotic impulses toward the women in the stationery stores where he seeks to make his purchase (one of these is Dupont's second wife, who may be Wallas' stepmother). Especially characteristic of the relationships between Robbe-Grilletian objects, which the author will exploit increasingly in later novels, is the establishment of both formal and *verbal* connections (though, of course, they remain implicit) between the *gomme* that haunts Wallas and the hard cube of lava that serves as a paperweight on (father) Dupont's desk. While the eraser is described as a "yellowish cube . . . with slightly rounded corners, as if from wear" the paperweight is depicted as "a sort of cube, but slightly deformed . . . with faces polished as if from wear, with rounded edges, compact, hard . . ." Two hundred pages later, when Wallas sees this cube again in the room where he will shortly kill Dupont, his vision imposes on the object aspects more in keeping with the mood of murder, and it is metamorphosed into "a cube of vitreous rock, with *sharp* edges and *murderous* corners."

Does the *gomme* also have an ideological meaning? Robbe-Grillet himself has spoken of "a little cube of rubber . . . which contains its own negation, the idea of erasure." This is surely evidence of a preoccupation with the theme of effacement, obliteration, and erasure that will recur in most of the later works, and of which the erasure of the spot left on the wall by the centipede of *Jealousy* is a striking example. Leon Roudiez has suggested that the *gomme* is intended to "erase" the theme of Oedipus from the novel, showing that myth is no longer relevant to modern man. Whatever view one takes, it must become obvious that strict *chosisme* is an inadequate concept with which to understand such objects. The proponents of neutral "things" in Robbe-Grillet failed to realize the extent of the influence of Sarte's ideas and examples. As *Nausea* had shown, and as Sarte had explained in his essays, human conscience, according to existentialist philosophy, can exist only by attaching itself to objects; in this way alone is

[17]

self-awareness possible. Thus the objects in Robbe-Grillet come into man's awareness as supports for his thoughts and emotions; they are more than objective correlatives, since they are necessary to, and cosubstantial with, his mental life. According to existentialist doctrine, the author of modern fiction must, to express the content of consciousness, attach himself to objects, rejecting the verbiage of psychological analysis, ideological commentary, and omniscient rumination, all of which will lie henceforth outside the novelistic field.

Thus *The Erasers,* despite many conventional techniques (such as the presentation of multiple points of view, some passages written from an omniscient angle as if spoken by a sort of transformed Greek chorus, the manipulation of an intricate and detailed plot, and the like), sounded a startling new note in contemporary fiction. Beneath its detective story were not only various levels of meaning (such as myth, psychic complex, and "object" semantics) but emergent novelistic techniques (such as objectified imagination, chronological distortions, topo-geometrical object descriptions, and formal series) which were shortly to reappear, in *The Voyeur,* and to continue their evolutionary development.

Perhaps the main structural link between *The Erasers* and *The Voyeur* (1955) is the use of a major ellipsis, or "hole" in the narrated action. In the former novel, the ellipse is the "crime" that precedes and sets in motion the rest of the work, the false murder of Dupont toward the realization of which the mechanism of the plot implacably moves, until what had been true only in the imaginings of the characters involved becomes "objectively" true. Though the characters in the novel are nearly all unaware of the elliptical event, the reader is not. In *The Voyeur,* however, the ellipse is total. Shortly after the novel begins, a "hole" in the action occurs. "Something" has happened, something that gradually acquires horrifying substance and form: the torture and murder of a young girl, thrown over the cliffs into the sea by the novel's protagonist, the sadistic psychopath Mathias. Robbe-Grillet has said of this structure: "Everything is told before the 'hole,' then again after the 'hole,' and there is an effort to bring together the two edges to eliminate this troublesome emptiness; but the opposite occurs, the 'hole' engulfs everything."

As is usually the case with Robbe-Grillet's works, critics differ radically in their interpretation of the crime of *The Voyeur*. Some deny its reality, some attribute it to someone other than Mathias, or even, in the case of Maurice Blanchot, to "time," whatever that may mean. The most straightforward reading, as well as that best supported by close scrutiny of the text, is that Mathias is indeed guilty, and that the coherence of the novel depends upon the step-by-step materialization and realization of this guilt and revelation of its psychological effects.

Disembarking on a coastal island unvisited since childhood (an echo of the same theme in *The Erasers*), a man designated only as "Mathias" or "the traveler" sets out on the latest of what is represented as a sad list of itinerant occupations. He has a satchel full of wrist watches to sell to the inhabitants. In order to cover the sinuous paths of the island, he rents a bicycle. Before setting out he imagines, in scenes that seem at first glance "real," several unsuccessful attempts to sell his wares. A number of themes related to voyeurism and sadism are stated, almost in leitmotiv style: a recollection of a violent scene observed through a window, in which a man was apparently beating or abusing a young girl; the erotic posture of another girl leaning against a mast of the ship; images of stout cords rolled in a figure-of-eight, the marks of iron rings on the sea wall, also having that shape, the flights of sea gulls whirling in patterns of eight. . . . (A full count of the "eight" forms of *The Voyeur* would include twenty or more similar designs scattered and interwoven throughout the novel.) Each act of Mathias, each contact with someone in a café or shop or street of the island, becomes a pretext for premonitory visual and psychic deformations suggestive of future violence. At a farmhouse where he at last sells a watch, he learns from his client that her young daughter Jacqueline is watching her sheep near a cliff to one side of the path he should take to reach the end of the island. When he arrives at the crossroads he turns his bicycle toward the cliffs and the sea. It is here that the "hole" in the action is found.

The narrative resumes about an hour later, with Mathias back at the point where the cliff path leaves the main road. Meeting Mme. Marek, a peasant woman who lives nearby, Mathias relates his "visit" to her farm. The attentive reader begins to suspect falsification. From this point on, the text increasingly takes on the atmosphere of repression, evasion, and a compulsive preoccupation with the establishment of an alibi for the missing hour. Mathias' lies are even doubled: the young Julien, Mme. Marek's son, "confirms" Mathias' false visit to the farm, thus covering his own *voyeur* presence at the scene on the cliff. When Mathias returns to this clearing, following the announcement of the finding of Jacqueline's body on the rocks off shore, Julien confronts him and shows him the clues that Mathias himself had hoped to recover (a cigarette butt and the wrapper from a bonbon). In a curious sort of connivance, Julien fails to denounce Mathias. Before Mathias leaves the island, unapprehended and unpunished, the image of the torture and killing of Jacqueline returns uncensored to his mind. It is the correspondence between this image and the "objective" events of the story, including the return to search for clues and the challenge by Julien, that constitutes the main justification for assuming the guilt of the protagonist.

It is probable that Robbe-Grillet's intention was to employ a single third-person point of view in *The Voyeur*, that of Mathias, a person "out of phase" with himself. Yet the text implies a divided point of view. The "split" in the hero's schizophrenic personality leads to a division between "objective" presentation by the author and "subjective" deformation of this created universe in Mathias' mind during the time (which becomes an increasingly large proportion of the text) when the protagonist's psychic turmoil converts the outside world into a systematic nightmare. Perhaps only a theoretical line separates the two techniques; but a number of scenes in which Mathias is viewed from a distance, or from an outside angle impossible to reconcile with the character's point of view, reinforce the impression that Robbe-Grillet has alternated less between the normal and abnormal vision of the same character than between his author's vision of the external world (already "stylized" *à la* Robbe-Grillet) and the interior imaginings and distortions brought about by the main character's psychopathological tensions. In fact, the freedom with which the text passes from exteriority to interiority, without boundaries or textual demarcations, provides one of the impressive effects of the novel, and prefigures the merging of real and imaginary scenes that will form the structural basis of later works such as *Last Year at Marienbad*.

As both Maurice Blanchot and John Weightman have observed, brilliance and luminosity pervade *The Voyeur*. Cliffs, waves, and gulls take on a new reality beneath a sun of laser-like intensity. Yet even the most "neutral" and innocent-seeming description of natural objects may contain, imperceptible at first glance but beyond a doubt fully intentional, some formal theme or coincidence of vocabulary that relates the object to the plot, or to the personality of Mathias, or to some aspect of a later action. For example, when Mathias looks around for a fixed point by which to judge the movement of his ship as it docks, his eyes fall upon "a mark in the shape of a figure-of-eight . . . two little circles, side by side, whose image remained in his mind," a mark left by an iron ring on the dock wall as it swung from side to side. This eight figure, like the others previously mentioned, is related to the theme of tying Jacqueline's wrists with the cord (rolled in an eight) found on deck, with the shape of eyeglasses and watching eyes (voyeurism), and with the whole elaborate system of eights and Y's that runs through the text. Even drawings and pictures described in the text are thus related, like so many Gide-like *constructions en abîme*, or interior duplications, to the main level of the novel: the picture of a man tearing apart a doll as its child owner cringes before him, a movie poster advertising "Monsieur X on the double track," a display card showing, at the focus of a ring of knives with open blades, a drawing representing "a tree with a svelte and straight trunk, terminating in two branches forming a Y, with a little tuft of foliage . . . at the hollow part of the fork," combining phallic symbolism with sado-erotic motifs. Elsewhere the complex period of small waves is described with seeming total objectivity: "two liquid masses, meeting each other, came together with the noise of a slap, and some drops of foam spurted up a little higher against the wall." Here the word *slap* goes beyond mere metaphor, preparing for and tying in with later scenes containing sadistic elements of slapping or beating.

The Voyeur also demonstrates the polyvalence of many of Robbe-Grillet's techniques and effects, devices that appear throughout his works yet are specifically related in each case to the individual structure of the particular fiction and to the "psychology" of its protagonist. The interrelated objects of *The Erasers* become the figure-of-eight series of *The Voyeur*, as appropriately integrated into Mathias' pathological personality as were the cubes of *The Erasers* to Wallas' Oedipal fixation. The hesitation and fear of the assassin Garinati in *The Erasers* were expressed in a "fixed" scene; Mathias' anxiety and feeling of forced waiting, until he can escape from the island, are embodied in a similar scene in which the movement of a sailor across the dock seems to cease each time Mathias glances away and resumes as he looks back, each time the sailor appearing as if setting out from the same spot at which he was last observed. Phrases broken into fragments recombined in apparent chaos communicated in *The Erasers* the confusion of the café proprietor as he was questioned by the police chief; in *The Voyeur* similar effects show evasions, blockings, repressions in Mathias' mind, or a compulsive echolalia that betrays an obsession, as when Mathias is unable to detach his attention from the picture of his victim ("the black note-book, the catalogues, the shiny metal frame containing the photograph, the photograph, the photograph, the photograph . . ."). "False" scenes, representing conjectures or hypotheses, consciously contrived by the characters in *The Erasers*, reappear in *The Voyeur* as almost hallucinatory embodiments of many of Mathias' psychopathological states.

For if a case can be made, as some critics would insist, for disregarding the implied "personality" of Mathias in *The Voyeur*, a far stronger case exists, surely, for seeing the entire novel as a carefully organized incarnation of attempted repression, in the mind of a schizoid protagonist, of a sadistic, erotic, murder. To those who say that a *voyeur* by definition does not commit a crime, but only watches, one may reply that Mathias is not necessarily the *voyeur* of the title, who may be instead the young Julien of the "odd glance," who has "seen all." Besides, may one not imagine a *voyeur* undergoing that "catathymic crisis" that plunges him into the irrevocable criminal act?

[23]

Robbe-Grillet's one novel that has no "objective" act of violence or crime is *Jealousy* (*La Jalousie*, 1957), regarded by many as his masterpiece. Oddly enough, an imaginary scene in which the jealous husband has a hallucinatory vision of a car wreck engulfing his wife and her putative lover in flames was misinterpreted by some as an overt scene of violence, leading, in one instance, to the strange reproach directed at the novel by the reviewer of *Time* magazine that the only "real" act of importance the work contained, a "murder," was dealt with in less than one page. No less curious was the mystification of certain readers concerning the presence or absence of a "narrator" in the text. Several French critics confessed that without the author's statement on the back cover of the novel they would not have realized that the entire text was the husband's "narration." In this *prière d'insérer*, Robbe-Grillet states clearly that the "narrator of this *récit*—a husband who exercises surveillance over his wife—is at the center of the plot, remaining there from the first sentence to the last." Using a unique form of narrative mode, that of the suppressed first person or *je-néant*, the author in a manner somewhat parallel to that of the "subjective camera" in the movies creates an unprecedented effect. Nowhere does any narrative pronoun or self reference appear; there is no "I," "me," or any self quotation, even in dialogues or conversations to which the husband is a party. The protagonist occupies what Robbe-Grillet calls a "hollow" in the middle of the text. The manipulation of the narrative mode causes the reader soon to install himself in this concavity, assuming the textual point of view, "becoming" the conscience of the narrator. The sensation of self-projection on the part of most readers is intense, and is essential to the complete functioning of the novel, since the "jealousy" implied in the title (which also refers to the type of sun blinds called *jalousies*) will be created in the reader, who undergoes, as it were, a direct experience of the fictional situation.

[24]

Jealousy is the first of Robbe-Grillet's works to be structured as a radically nonchronological matrix of events. As the author notifies his readers, "This irreducible narrator, always present, cannot be concerned with chronology; every scene is for him present, or lost. His field of perception constitutes the universe, *here* and *now*." Since this "field of perception" includes not only "real" episodes, unfolding at the moment of narration, but also reiterated and often dynamically deformed memories, anticipations, imaginations, and hallucinations, the text becomes a kind of psychic magma in which events and objects come and go, sink and surge up, disappear and return to form new patterns or relationships. In his use of thematic returns, variations, associative modulations, and linkings, Robbe-Grillet in *Jealousy* parallels many features of musical structure. Inner psychic unity governs the order of events and their *reprises* to such an extent that the most careful attempt to "reconstruct" their real or external order meets with chronological impasses (as will be the case later in *Marienbad* and *L'Immortelle*). One can, however, identify a main plot movement, which runs from the inception and gradual intensification of suspicions in the mind of the planter-narrator concerning his young wife "A . . ." through his emotional crisis during the absence of "A . . .," who has left for a trip to the coast with the aggressively masculine Franck (supervisor of an adjacent banana plantation), to the gradual appeasement of suspicions, or cessation of active resentment against Franck, following the return from the coastal trip and the evident coolness that now prevails between "A . . ." and Franck.

This brief, intense triangular plot, which is unconventional only in its lack of an objective denouement, unfolds entirely within the rectangle of a tropical plantation house whose corner posts cast on the wide three-sided porch sundial-like shadows marking the time of day and cutting the action into slices. At the cocktail hour, "A . . ." and Franck sit side by side behind the husband's chair, placed forward toward the view of the valley in an "arrangement that forces anyone sitting there to make extreme rotations of the head if he wishes to see A . . . ." Franck and "A . . ." discuss a novel they are reading, which seems to involve an unfaithful wife in an African setting. One evening at dinner a centipede runs up the wall opposite "A . . .," who seems electrified at the sight. Franck gets up and crushes it with his napkin, leaving an ugly spot. Later, when ice is lacking on the terrace, the narrator (one might almost say, the *text*) leaves to get some, pausing to look out through the *jalousies* in a vain attempt to see what Franck and "A . . ." do in the meantime. When the ice is brought, a letter has appeared protruding from Franck's pocket, and it is shortly thereafter, no doubt, that "A . . ." announces her intention of accompanying Franck on his next trip to the coast, in order to do some "shopping." Yet fragments of events that must occur much "later" in any real chronology have already made their appearance in the text. Intercalated among scenes preceding the departure are portions of scenes of "A . . .'s" return, as well as allusions to the explanation she gives for staying overnight at the coast (a breakdown of Franck's car).

Thus by the time the reader reaches parts 6 and 7 of the nine that form the book, and begins the climactic experience of the night of waiting for "A . . .'s" return, all the elements and themes have been stated. What is remarkable is that instead of diminishing the effect of suspense this foreknowledge of future events increases the tension. It is now that the magnifications and distortions of the narrator's jealous imagination reach their paroxysm. The episode of the centipede returns magnified and frighteningly charged with erotic meaning; from an insect of "normal size" in the earlier scenes it has become transformed into a "gigantic creature . . . [with] its antennae extended, its immense legs spread out around its body, covering almost the surface area of a plate. . . ." When Franck kills it with his *serviette*, the word itself takes on another meaning, that of a hand towel, which Franck "replaces on the metal towel rack, near the washstand," as he "returns to the bed" where "A . . ." awaits him behind a torn mosquito netting. This hallucinatory, agonized image of the lovers *flagrante delicto* is then transformed through ambiguous verbal linkings, such as "haste to reach his goal," "Franck accelerates his pace," and "the movements become more violent," into a vision of Franck's car as it crashes against a rigid tree. "Flames" then spring up and "illuminate the thick shrubbery," and in the crackling of the fire the husband hears "the noise of the centipede, once more motionless on the wall," making a noise that "sounds like breathing as much as like crackling," or like the sound of "A . . .'s" brush being stroked down along undone hair. The reference to "A . . .'s" brushing her hair joins to this complex objectification of tortured jealousy still another thematic scene repeated often in the text.

Is the centipede of *Jealousy* an erotic symbol? Is it an objective correlative expressing the husband's jealous fear that his wife is possessed by another man? Or does it have a different function? Robbe-Grillet would no doubt call it psychic "support" of passionate emotion. To argue over terminology only obscures the issue. It is plainly evident that the husband's jealousy *exists in* the centipede images. According to Sartrian existentialist phenomenology, consciousness can only be awareness *of* something other than itself. Consciousness without the objects of the world outside to attach itself to is nonexistent. Robbe-Grillet's depictions of *things* that serve as the focus of his protagonist's consciousness, taking on the appearances and relationships conferred on them by the character's psychic projections, thus convey not only the visual "mental content" of the narrator but also his emotional life. Analysis and commen-

[27]

tary are no longer desirable, or necessary; nowhere in the novel is there a single *reference* to jealousy (except for the pun on *la jalousie*), suspicion, infidelity, or anything of the sort (excepting, perhaps, the allusions that "A . . ." and Franck make to the plot of the "inner novel" they are reading). A description of the proximity of the hands of "A . . ." and Franck, sitting in their chairs, suffices to *create* suspicion, not only in the narrator (who does not give it a name) but in the participating reader. Even such controversial passages as the tedious counting of the banana trees in a trapezoidal field have psychic meaning: here, the husband's meticulous habits of observation, symptomatic of a withdrawn, perhaps impotent personality, could be advanced to "explain" the incident. Similarly, his paranoia (associated in manuals of psychopathology with excessive attention to details) may "explain" various other series of minutely depicted objects in serial forms (such as *V*'s), spots of various kinds and degrees (the stain left by the centipede, the oil stain in the parking area behind the house, the blood-red ink spot on a wall, and so on) that relate to the theme of *erasure*, as in the attempt to remove the centipede spot with a gum eraser and razor blade.

Jealousy has been called a "cinematographic" novel. The textbook edition used in American college courses actually contains a "special vocabulary" of cinema terms used by the editors in their discussion and notes. Critics have sought to identify the narrative mode with that of the subjective camera employed in Robert Montgomery's film *Lady in the Lake*, in which the lens of a camera strapped to the protagonist's chest films each scene as if viewed by a person behind the camera, in the position of the spectator. Many of *Jealousy*'s linkings employ cinematic transformations of objects and associative fondus, or dissolves (for example, a chair in a photograph of "A . . ." becomes a real chair on the terrace). Although it seems legitimate to make certain analogies of this kind, the technique of *liaison des scènes*, which gives continuity to *Jealousy*, is in reality much more complicated, going beyond visual transitions comparable to those of the movies into the realm of verbal, auditory, and above all implicit psychic associations conveyed by essentially literary means. Despite its resemblance, especially in retrospect, to Robbe-Grillet's films, *Jealousy* was, and remains, a *novel*.

To many critics, Robbe-Grillet's next (and to this date his last) novel, *In the Labyrinth* (1959) marked a change of direction, if not a metamorphosis, in his work. Of all his novels and films, it is by far the nearest approach to the *roman pur*. In the "pure" novel, Flaubert once stated, the artist would create a "book about nothing, a book without exterior connections." The aesthetic value of such a novel would lie in its form alone, and in the "articulations" holding it together. According to Robbe-Grillet, *In the Labyrinth* was conceived somewhat along these Flaubertian lines. It was to be a novel in which the basic formal conception of an *écriture labyrinthine*—a style that would move forward to an impasse, retreat, pursue another course, encounter a further blocking, and take a new direction, until finally a momentary issue or exit appeared—would cause the work to create its own fictional reality.

As if to emphasize this coherence of style and story, the author warns his readers that the book is only a fiction with "no allegorical meaning" whose reality contained nothing beyond the "things, gestures, words, and events" of the text. This "strictly material reality," which has no more or less meaning "than the reader's own life, or his death," is of course different from ordinary reality, since it is created within the work and thus remains, in Flaubert's phrase, "without exterior connec-

[29]

tions." Yet, ironically, of all Robbe-Grillet's novels, *In the Labyrinth* has been the one most often considered allegorical; and its objects, especially the mysterious box carried by the soldier, have been variously interpreted as (even religious!) symbols.

The geometric, mazelike city of the novel, with its streets in parallels and right angles, its identical houses, its endless perspective of wrought-iron lamp posts, recalls that of *The Erasers*, except for the absence of canals and bridges. But instead of constituting, as in the earlier work, a décor within whose *être-là*, or "thereness," the events and characters of the story exist, the city of *In the Labyrinth*, with its characters, "materializes" within the sentences of the text itself. Employing an unusual narrative mode, Robbe-Grillet gives us a narrator or pseudo-narrator who says "I" in the novel's first sentence and "my" toward the last pages of the work. This narrator is installed in a closed room high above the street, a room whose floor is marked by paths left by shuffling slippers, whose walls are papered in a design resembling, among other things, falling snow. The room also contains various future "objects" of the story (a bayonet, a box) as well as an engraving entitled "The Defeat at Reichenfels," showing a café crowded with the very characters, including the soldier protagonist, whose actions will fill most of the novel.

The first appearance of the soldier (who is a second narrator, or the narrator's *alter ego*) illustrates Robbe-Grillet's technique of literary materialization. The "I" narrator in his room has been examining the image of an electric light filament cast on the wall by a tiny hole in the lamp shade. A cinematic transition occurs, in which the outline of a street lamp post and the soldier are traced, so to speak, by the sentences of the text:

It is again the same filament, one of a light bulb of the same size or a little larger, that shines uselessly at the street intersection, enclosed in its glass cage at the top of an iron standard, an old gas light with outdated curves and ornaments that has become an electric light post.

Against the conical base of the iron support, with its slight convexity at the bottom, and surrounded by several more or less prominent rings, are entwined the thin branches of a theoretical ivy pattern, in relief: undulating stems, pointed five-lobed leaves with their five obvious veins, on which the peeling black paint has become detached from the rusty metal. Somewhat higher up, a hip, an arm, a shoulder lean against the lamp post. The man is clothed in a military coat of a doubtful color, faded, between green and khaki. His face is gray. . . .

It is seemingly this same soldier who may be seen, with the box that he carries, in the Reichenfels engraving. The minute description of this picture (some six pages in length) gradually turns into the depiction of an animated scene, and the microcosmic image on the narrator's wall expands to constitute the full reality of the text.

Lost in the city, searching for a street whose name he cannot recall, carrying a box that he must turn over to someone he does not know, this soldier, hungry, tired, and ill, seeks to fulfill his mission before the enemy, already victorious, arrives to occupy the town. A small boy guides him, in contradictory stages, to the café that forms one of the "foci" of the labyrinth. Elsewhere a young woman takes him in and feeds him. Images of the soldier blend with a photograph of the woman's husband, and an ambiguous limping man, whose presence frightens the young woman, begins an insistent surveillance of the soldier's movements. Silently, snow falls on the city, and the crisscross of tracks left by passing feet reinforces the feeling of feverish confusion. The soldier spends a night in a clandestine refuge for lost soldiers; he searches for his boy guide in apartment house corridors that form an inner labyrinth. Wounded by an advance detachment of enemy soldiers, the soldier is again taken in by the young woman, to whom he gives the package. The narrator, to whose room the text has retreated periodically, arrives in the guise of a doctor. He witnesses the soldier's death and receives from the woman the box that now lies on the mantelpiece of his room (as at the beginning of the novel). Abandoning the "scattered pages" lying on his table, the narrator leaves the room and the whole city "behind me," and the novel ends.

But not before the narrator lists his inventory of the box: some ordinary soldier's letters, a cheap watch, a ring, a bayonet blade. All these had belonged to a wounded comrade who had asked the soldier-protagonist to deliver them to someone, perhaps his father, in the city. The "neutral" contents of the box struck some readers as a disappointment, since the box had become highly charged with mystery and suspense. Seekers of allegories saw it as a sort of casket for the soldier's soul, a symbol reinforced by the role of the narrator as a "doctor" (and therefore a sort of priest). By his deliberate "demystification" of the contents of the box, Robbe-Grillet no doubt wished to emphasize the nonallegorical, nonsymbolic "material reality" of the text. It may be pointed out that the medieval novelist Chrétien de Troyes left unexplained many enigmatic objects and characters that appeared in his works. Dissatisfied, however, with these uninterpretable, or at least uninterpreted, symbols, Chrétien's readers supplied the most diverse meanings to his lances, silver bowls, and Fisher Kings.

In setting up barriers against symbolic or metaphysical interpretations for *In the Labyrinth*, Robbe-Grillet has at the same time given us, in the Mallarméan sense, a work that is "allegorical of itself." A narrator, shut up in a room where, sitting before the blank page, he is to create a work, assembles his elements: the tracks on the floor, the bayonet on the mantelpiece, the snowlike wallpaper design, the engraving on the wall showing some earlier scene of a military defeat and its effect on the townspeople gathered in a café. Tortuously, he pursues the creative pattern, which leads to impasses, new tentatives, new impasses, other solutions. Strict chronology disappears, geometry is distorted, characters become double (at one point the soldier sees himself elsewhere in the street). Style and form pursue their creative materialization of objects and events. The aim of the novel is nothing more, and nothing less, than to create itself in its own realization. Not only does its teleology lie *within*, but the design of the work is to a large extent free of the implicit psychological motivations essential to the structure of *The Voyeur* or *Jealousy*. What is quite remarkable is that *In the Labyrinth*, far from constituting a cold, intellectual exercise in self-fulfillment, has a lyrical, moving pathos not duplicated elsewhere in Robbe-Grillet's novels.

It was to be expected that Robbe-Grillet's film *Last Year at Marienbad* (1961) would demonstrate the latent cinematic content or technique of his previous works, and in fact it did so, though most critics failed to perceive the continuity of form and style. Some wrote as if the movie *Marienbad* were a complete reversal or abandonment of everything Robbe-Grillet had invented in his novels. In an attempt to refute this view, the present author (in his study of *Les Romans de Robbe-Grillet*) wrote this synthetic comparison:

Last Year at Marienbad may be seen as the prolongation and outcome of Robbe-Grillet's novelistic techniques, accompanied by, or transformed into, cinematographic procedures which reinforce them and bring them to fuller development. False scenes and objectified hypotheses as in *The Voyeur*, a subjective universe converted into objective perceptions as in *Jealousy*—with its detemporalization of mental states, its mixture of memories (true and false), of desire images and affective projections—the "dissolves" found in *The Labyrinth:* all these reach a high point in *Marien-*

[33]

bad. . . . The spectator's work, like that of the reader, becomes an integral part of the cinematic or novelistic creation. The "time of the reader" which José-María Castellet announced for the new novel becomes the "time of the spectator" for the new cinema.

That the viewer of *Marienbad* was expected to collaborate in creating the meaning of the film became evident in the reactions of critics and public. The question of what happens in the movie, and of what "had happened" problematically last year at Marienbad or in some other baroque mid-European château converted into a luxury hotel, became the subject of so many conjectures that Bernard Pingaud drew up a list of the various "grids" that could be placed upon the action, leading to some eight or ten interpretations. Nowhere in Robbe-Grillet's work is the question of the degree of reality of what is present on the screen (or in the text), so acutely raised as in *Marienbad;* yet this difficulty pales beside the greater dilemma of deciding what kind of reality, or lack of it, should be assigned to the real or imaginary past, which the hero and heroine affirm or deny, allude to or suppress, remember or imagine, create or destroy. Granted that this "virtual" action cannot have the reality or presence of what one sees on the screen (as Robbe-Grillet points out in a perhaps oversimplified attempt to dismiss as nonexistent whatever is not shown), it nevertheless forms part of the implied content of the film, since one's attitude toward it determines in large measure one's reactions to the main characters' behavior and one's interpretation of their "mental content," which the author himself has identified as the true subject of the film.

As the movie *Marienbad* begins, a voice speaks and the camera "subjectively" moves through the corridors and empty rooms of an ornate Bavarian palace. "Once more," the voice insists, in each description or comment, the unseen narrator's steps advance, "as before, toward you." When the camera arrives in front of a small stage, a play is in progress; the narrator's voice speaks for the male character, who seeks to lead away a reluctant heroine. Then the voice changes. A "real" actor now speaks, the play ends, the lights go on. In the animated, mundane atmosphere of dances, games (including the notorious "jeu de Marienbad" played with matches), walks in formal gardens among allegorical statues and hedges, intimate small rooms for private talks, stairways, and corridors (above all, those "Freudian" corridors!), the hero, indicated in the printed text as X, insistently pursues the heroine, A, a young woman obviously watched jealously by an older man, M (suggesting "*mari*" or husband). Despite A's denials, X continues to describe their love affair of last year, including A's promise to decide, in the year's interval, whether to leave with X. Gradually, A's denials become weaker, but not before we have witnessed, in those "mental content" scenes that take us inside her mind, as well as inside that of X, phantasies of seduction and resistance, desire and fear, rape, and even murder. Finally, as the film draws to a close, A, in apparent dejection and defeat, allows herself to be led away by X, whose voice resumes as at the beginning, but now referring to the couple's departure in the *past* tense.

The circularity of the film (emphasized by the "once more" of the beginning, and the past tense of the end) suggests that the author intended the same kind of re-entry of the end into the beginning that one finds, for example, in Joyce's *Finnegans Wake*. In this sense, nothing "exists" outside the film itself, last year is this year; the only reality is the here and now of the film's ninety minutes. All perspectives into another time or place are illusory, occurring only in the characters' minds. The spectator is not to concern himself with any "external" connections, or to speculate, as nearly everyone did, as to whether "last year" really existed. Claude Mauriac has insisted that it is

[35]

impossible not to speculate thus, and it is well known that Alain Resnais, who shot the film, prepared an elaborate chronological table of the scenes, placing them at various levels of time and reality, including a Monday to Saturday "last year" sequence, a Tuesday to Sunday "present" series, with first- and second-degree flashbacks, as well as scenes lying in a "timeless" zone outside any chronological schematic. Claude Ollier framed a "level of reality" scheme of images, ranging from "real" scenes to memory-images, desire-images, and false-memory-images. Since Robbe-Grillet explicitly stresses in his preface his view that the cinema is especially well adapted to the showing of mental content, it seems impossible to view *Marienbad* apart from this conception, especially since it derives, as we have seen, from the false and imaginary scene techniques of his earlier works.

Admitting the "open" nature of the film, can one explain it satisfactorily within its own framework? Two solutions may be proposed. We may assume A to be an exceptionally, even pathologically suggestible person, who is gradually overcome by the profuse insistence of X and his systematic efforts at persuasion. Though perhaps unlikely, this is not impossible, as shown by case histories given in works like Dr. Grasset's *Hypnotism and Suggestion*, which contains some really remarkable parallels to incidents in *Marienbad*. Or we may view the film as another materialization of the creative process, similar to that of *In the Labyrinth*, in which X is a sort of author or creative artist who forges a new truth or reality from the raw materials of his imagination. *Marienbad* would then be "his" novel.

Whatever theory one may adopt, the main interest of the work lies in its scenes and structure. All the Robbe-Grilletian art of transitions and scene-linking practiced in the novels returns in cinematic form. Interior duplications (the inner play,

[36]

thematic snatches of conversation stating many elements of the plot, doubling of events and characters) abound with telling effect. Chronological deformations, including one notable technique of the rotating camera which returns to characters already shown, but now in different postures and locations physically and temporally "impossible," distort both the "present" and the "past." A's room, shown first in its "normal" form, is later changed into an excessively ornate, baroque image by the heroine's tortured emotional state. It is in this room that one of the most memorable scenes of the film occurs: a confrontation between what A imagines and what X says to her, as if he could see within her mind and carry into that imaginary realm his persuasive struggle against her terrified resistance. "You came back to the bed," X tells her, repeatedly, as she flees from the bedroom in which she has mentally placed herself in response to X's words. In such structures as these, previous conceptions of point of view would seem to require modification, since we are obviously here confronted by an amalgam of viewpoints, both real and imaginary, and both simultaneously present. Yet, despite the free passage from one point of view to another, there is certainly no "omniscient narrator" in the nineteenth-century, Balzacian sense. The narrator becomes the spectator, as it were. We enter into a fictional realm of externalized imagination. *Marienbad*, therefore, goes beyond the simple objectification of mental content, real or false; it creates new patterns of aesthetic reality demanding new methods of analysis and new criteria of appreciation.

Robbe-Grillet's next film, *L'Immortelle* (1963), begins with a thematic prelude, some twenty shots announcing the key episodes and scenes to follow: a car crash on a road outside Istanbul, a young woman seen in various postures and locations, a man—the protagonist or "narrator," N—looking out through slanting sun blinds (*jalousies*), a Turkish cemetery, a fortress tower, a wharf with a fisherman, a white convertible with the top down, a heavy-set Turk wearing dark glasses and flanked by two huge dogs. If one views these prelude shots as a series of "parentheses" (in a style reminiscent of Raymond Roussel's multiple inner parentheses in *Nouvelles Impressions d'Afrique*, a work much admired by Robbe-Grillet), the scene with N looking through the nearly closed Venetian blinds may perhaps be the real point of departure, so that the film may be considered to begin *after* the meeting of N with the heroine L (for any of her various names, Lâle, Leïla, Lia . . .).

At any rate, the film, following the prelude, moves to a deceptively conventional beginning: a sequence in which the hero, a professor who has just arrived in Istanbul for a year's stay, loses his way along the Bosporus and pauses to ask directions from a young woman standing near, yet apart from, a Turk in dark glasses who is seemingly preoccupied with his two great dogs. The young woman offers to drive N home in her white convertible, listens to his account of himself, and agrees to come to a small gathering of friends in his apartment overlooking the water.

N's sudden and violent preoccupation with L pervades the sequence devoted to this gathering, and provokes a number of "unreal" or impossible shots, with the camera oscillating from right to left and back again, showing changes in décor and objects that disappear or undergo subtle alterations. There follows a long series of shots showing various meetings, excursions, shopping trips, and love episodes between N and L. N's extreme curiosity concerning L's identity remains unsatisfied; she appears and disappears, never revealing her situation in life or her address. In the background, ambiguous characters who seem to be spying on them—including a fisherman in front of N's house, a salesman in an antique shop where N purchases a statuette for L, a small boy, and the ominous Turk with his dogs—create an atmosphere of tension reflected from time to time in the nervous, fearful reactions of L. The lovers meet in an abandoned cemetery, in a mosque (whose guardian may be a "counterspy" who whispers secret information to L), in a park (where L laughingly throws away the paper on which she has written a "false" address), at N's apartment. Here L performs an erotic dance like the one the two have witnessed in a cabaret; but when N awkwardly lifts his hand to her throat in a stiff caress, L's face is contracted with fear. Later, when the two are visiting a ruined castle, the small boy brings L a message (in Greek) that "he" has returned; L leaves immediately, promising to meet N in the Turkish cemetery.

But N waits in vain; night falls; the lights of passing cars at one moment illuminate M (the Turk) and his dogs. Now begins N's first search for L: he recovers the notebook page on which L pretended to write her address (it is blank); he questions a woman guest present at the gathering, whose evasive replies provoke a recall of the original scene, this time with appreciable differences in L's behavior, suggesting connivance or an exchange of secrets with the woman whom L had pretended to know only slightly. N's return to the antique shop leads to similar repetitions of earlier shots. At last, after fruitless interviews in various quarters of the city, N sees L, at night, standing near M and his dogs. He leads her forcibly away, and the two get into L's car.

Still refusing to explain her actions, L drives faster and faster, with N at her side, along the Bosporus road. Suddenly, one of M's dogs looms in the headlights. L (or N) turns the wheel violently, and the car crashes. L dies instantly of a broken neck, while N suffers only a scratched hand.

N, now wearing a bandage on his injured hand, undertakes a new search for L's identity, as if impelled by posthumous jealousy. About a third of the film is devoted to this mixture of "new" scenes (N with his hand bandaged) and "old" ones already witnessed once or twice (but now further distorted by N's jealous scrutiny). Some scenes thus return for the third time, since N had already recalled them during his earlier re-examination of the past. Now the increased emotional intensity of N raises them (as happens in the repeated scenes of the novel *Jealousy*) to an even higher level of implied psychological meaning. The night scene in the car becomes an outright hallucination: N with his hand bandaged sees L sitting beside him, her face contorted with terror. Implied notions of imprisonment, of L as a sort of slave perhaps beaten by some powerful and jealous man (M, or someone whose agent M is), are suggested by images of L standing as if chained to a wall, or views of barred windows. In a paroxysm of erotic memory, N sees a lascivious L writhing before him in an ecstasy of desire and fear. Discovering in a junkyard a white car resembling L's, N buys it and sets out on a second wild nocturnal drive along the Bosporus road where L had met her death. L's voice urges him to drive faster. M's second dog looms in the headlights. The car crashes, and N dies in a posture identical to that of L in the first crash. A coda of shots reintroduces, as in the prelude, various scenes with L, whose silent laughter accompanies the film's final images.

Such a résumé shows the basically simple anecdotal armature on which *L'Immortelle* is constructed: a man tortured by jealousy seeks to discover the identity of a woman with whom he has a brief, intense love affair, only to die in an accident similar to the one that has killed her. In comparison with *Marienbad*, the plot is closer to ordinary experience; there is no problematic "last year," no implication of cyclic repetitions or of a possible allegory of death. Nor does Robbe-Grillet resort to camera devices to mark scenes as more or less "real" (as Resnais had done with the "white" scenes of *Marienbad*, which are not so designated in the written scenario). As Robbe-Grillet says, the cinema can give images of mental content without identifying the scenes as such. Much of the ambiguity of *Marienbad* depends on the spectator's uncertainty as to whether a given scene is supposed to take place "inside the head" of the hero or the heroine. *L'Immortelle* remains fairly consistently "with" the hero, never presenting L's mental images (although the film occasionally adopts briefly the point of view of a "spy," of M, or of a kind of disembodied observer, who may be N looking at himself and L from the "outside"). Some scenes use the subjective camera (with the lens where N's eyes would be), but in most instances the camera is *alongside* N. The actor who played N (Doniol-Valcroze) "suppressed" all show of emotion, using a stiff, impassive acting style. The effect, correctly understood, is to detract attention from N, as a person does in recalling his own experiences, and to focus attention on L or whatever N regards; it is a means, without resorting to the exclusive use of subjective camera (which, as *Lady in the Lake* demonstrated, cannot maintain the desired effect), of subjectifying the narration while retaining the third-person mode.

The transitions that give coherence to the film are, as in most of Robbe-Grillet's works, formal and associative. The art with which these are manipulated to permit the shifts from present to past, from reality to deformed memory, imagination, and hallucination, makes *L'Immortelle* in both texture and form a masterpiece of construction. Correlative objects, thematic linkings, integrated repetitions—all impose on the conventional order of beginning, middle, and end a different structural pattern, based somewhat on the principle of *entrelacement* as used by medieval authors like Chrétien de Troyes, wherein serial arrangements, recall of earlier episodes, repetitions, and complicated interlocking shifts and intercalated story elements seem to yield an endless, circular pattern not necessarily directed toward a final conclusion. But the Aristotelian, "teleological" form triumphs finally, when death brings a feeling of appeasement and a relaxation of tension by putting an end to the emotional crisis of the film's protagonist.

Objects in *L'Immortelle* undergo a number of metamorphoses that show a close analogy to the evolution of such things as the *scutigère*, or centipede, of *Jealousy*—which is converted by the husband's psychic obsessions into a monstrous, threatening enormity—or the heroine's bedroom in *Marienbad*, with its increasingly baroque ornamentation and proliferation of "irrealist" details (like the multiplication of the photograph given her by X as "proof" of their former liaison). For example, N's bandaged hand is seen at one point rummaging through his desk drawer, searching among old letters and papers, Turkish bank notes, souvenir post cards, and other anodyne, "innocent" items found there. Suddenly, the hand encounters an object highly charged with fetish-like erotic meaning: a black lace garter. Immediately N's mind reverts to L's Oriental dance, which she again performs, this time pushing its eroticism to the farthest limit of the film. There is a *stretto* of brief shots of L in various seminude postures, culminating in a scene in which N's hand (unbandaged) caresses her neck in an ambiguous, sado-erotic gesture. The next shot again shows the drawer, open, but now N's emotional stress, which in this retrospective phase of his jealousy has led him to the borders of hallucination and beyond, causes him to see therein (as the audience now witnesses on the screen at a completely "realistic" level) not merely the harmless, everyday items the drawer contained before, but, intruding among and almost obscuring them, such menacing objects as a vicious-looking curved knife,

[42]

a heavy iron ring resembling part of a pair of handcuffs, and "a large number of gum erasers." N's hand clenches, in a strangling gesture. The past is here not only brought into the present, but intensified and made an active force of psychic distortion effecting a change in N's vision of the world. Since all these shots occur without the usual soft-focus blurring or other cinematographic "clues" to subjective passages, the effect on the spectator is startling and powerful.

L'Immortelle contains, as had *The Erasers, In the Labyrinth,* and, to some extent, *Marienbad,* sets of Robbe-Grilletian *doubles*. Like all interior duplications these serve (as Gide once pointed out) to intensify the meaning of the story at the level of the characters themselves. They also permit, or encourage, the spectator to envision other "possibilities" of plot development: false, or parallel story lines. A man in dark glasses wearing clothes like M's emerges from the mosque where N is waiting for L; he stares at N and L in a cabaret; on N's first search for L he is sent to a house seemingly owned by this "double" of M. The "other" M is seen, toward the end of the film, sitting beside a woman resembling L and playing with two great dogs, in a scene duplicating N's first encounter with L. L's double plays an even greater role: N follows her in his search for the "real" L, comes upon her eying him fearfully from a barred window, and even hears from her, on the street, a deformed version of his own story and that of the "real" L. Minor characters also undergo permutations of their roles: the fisherman-spy posted in front of N's house becomes a pastry vendor, then a fish merchant, while a different pastry vendor becomes the postcard seller at the mosque who gives secret information to L in a language not understood by N. At least once, N and L "double" for themselves in a panoramic shot of disturbing effect.

[43]

Thus, Robbe-Grillet's latest film continues the evolution of novelistic and cinematographic forms that mark his work since its inception, and at the same time points to new developments for the cinema of the future. This new cinema will not only attach itself to and express "mental reality," according to the system of projected interiority that Robbe-Grillet has repeatedly defended on grounds of realistic psychology (that of "our loves, our affective life"). It will also deal with *created* subjective truth. It will be a cinema of forms, which will increasingly reveal its richest meaning in the modalities and contours of these forms themselves. "Homme nouveau, nouveau roman," Robbe-Grillet has written. If contemporary man requires a "new novel" to fit his new situation (ideological, psychological, sociological, or whatever), must he not forge a new cinema as well? It would be a serious error to believe that because Robbe-Grillet's works contain human psychology, they are only disguised versions of conventional novel and film forms inherited from the past. From past styles, including his own, Robbe-Grillet causes, with astonishing ingenuity, previously unknown forms and structures to emerge, and creates, with and through them, new psychic experiences. As a result, man is enabled to enter uncharted domains of fiction in search of a new reality which he can only attain through works of art.

Is it too early to elevate Robbe-Grillet to the status of a modern master? He has said himself that another ten years will be required to show whether the current interest in his work is a transitory phenomenon, due perhaps to a kind of snobbism, or a recognition of durable artistic achievement. It is surely not too early to affirm that, whatever value future critics may set upon his achievement, his novels and films have already strongly influenced the post World War II generation of novelists and scenarists. If, as Valéry once said of Mallarmé, the strongest proof of a poet's importance is that no later poet could write poetry as if he had not existed, then Robbe-Grillet's importance is already intensely felt. Literary criticism of his works is currently proliferating. Robbe-Grillet has recently placed himself frankly in the Stendhal-Balzac-Flaubert-Proust-Gide tradition. Is this too ambitious? For the moment, it would seem that it is not. To moderns, Robbe-Grillet is a master creator. Readers and critics unconcerned with posterity's eventual support or reversal of their judgment will ask nothing more. In the mid-1960s, Alain Robbe-Grillet appears to many to stand at the most advanced point of evolution of the twentieth-century novel and film.

SELECTED BIBLIOGRAPHY

NOTE: *The translations of Robbe-Grillet's works into English are all by Richard Howard, except as indicated. Only critical studies in English have been listed, and these are limited to nonjournalistic articles treating aspects of his work in some depth and detail. Readers of French are referred to the text and bibliography of the present author's study,* Les Romans de Robbe-Grillet, *Paris, Minuit, 1963.*

PRINCIPAL WORKS OF ALAIN ROBBE-GRILLET

Les Gommes. Paris, Minuit, 1953. (The Erasers. New York, Grove Press, 1964.)

Le Voyeur. Paris, Minuit, 1955. (The Voyeur. New York, Grove Press, 1958.)

La Jalousie. Paris, Minuit, 1957. (Jealousy. New York, Grove Press, 1959.)

Dans le Labyrinthe. Paris, Minuit, 1959. (In the Labyrinth. New York, Grove Press, 1960.)

L'Année dernière à Marienbad, ciné-roman. Paris, Minuit, 1961. (Last Year at Marienbad. New York, Grove Press, 1962.)

Instantanés. Paris, Minuit, 1962. (Portions in English: "The Shore," *London Magazine*, Vol. 5, No. 4 (April, 1958); "The Way Back," *London Magazine*, Vol. 6, No. 12 (December, 1959); "Scene," *Big Table*, No. 5 [Tr. Bruce Morrissette]. "Three Reflected Visions," *Evergreen Review*, Vol. 1, No. 3 [Tr. Richard Howard]."The Secret Room," *Esquire*, February, 1963 [Tr. not credited].)

L'Immortelle, ciné-roman. Paris, Minuit, 1963.

Pour un Nouveau Roman. Paris, Minuit, 1963. (Portions in English: "A Fresh Start for Fiction," *Evergreen Review*, Vol. 1, No. 3; "Old 'Values' and the New Novel," *Evergreen Review*, Vol. 3, No. 9 [Tr. Bruce Morrissette].)

CRITICAL WORKS AND COMMENTARY

Alter, Jean V. "The Treatment of Time in Alain Robbe-Grillet's *La Jalousie," College Language Association Journal*, Vol. 3 (September, 1959).

[46]

Barnes, Hazel. "The Ins and Outs of Robbe-Grillet," *Chicago Review*, Vol. 15, No. 3 (Winter, 1961–62).

Brée, Germaine. "New Blinds or Old?," *Yale French Studies* ("Midnight Novelists" issue), No. 24 (1959).

Champigny, Robert. "In Search of the Pure Récit," *American Society Legion of Honor Magazine*, Vol. 27 (Winter, 1956–57).

Dort, Bernard. "Are These Novels Innocent?," *Yale French Studies* ("Midnight Novelists" issue), No. 24 (1959).

Gilman, Richard. "Total Revolution in the Novel," *Horizon* (January, 1962).

Girard, René. "Pride and Passion in the Contemporary Novel," *Yale French Studies* ("Midnight Novelists" issue), No. 24 (1959).

Giraud, Raymond. "Unrevolt among the Unwriters in France Today," *Yale French Studies* ("Midnight Novelists" issue), No. 24 (1959).

LeSage, Laurent. The French New Novel. University Park, Pa., Pennsylvania State University Press, 1962.

Loy, Robert J. "*Things* in Recent French Literature," *PMLA*, Vol. 71 (March, 1956).

Morrissette, Bruce. "New Structure in the Novel: *Jealousy* by Robbe-Grillet," *Evergreen Review*, Vol. 3, No. 10 (1959).

——— "Oedipus and Existentialism: *Les Gommes* of Robbe-Grillet," *Wisconsin Studies in Contemporary Literature*, Vol. 1, No. 3 (Fall, 1960).

——— "The New Novel in France," *Chicago Review*, Vol. 15, No. 3 (Winter–Spring 1961–62).

Mudrick, Marvin. "A Warning to Optimists," *Hudson Review* (1960).

Peyre, Henri. "Trends in the Contemporary French Novel," in New French Writing. Ed. Georges Borchardt. New York, Criterion, 1961.

Pingaud, Bernard. "The School of Refusal," *Yale French Studies* ("Midnight Novelists" issue), No. 24 (1959).

Roudiez, Leon S. "The Embattled Myths," in *Hereditas*. Ed. Frederic Will. Austin, Tex., Texas University Press, 1964.

Stoltzfus, Ben F. Alain Robbe-Grillet and the New French Novel. Carbondale, Ill., Southern Illinois Press, 1964.

Tyler, Parker. "Robbe-Grillet," *University of Houston Quarterly* (Fall, 1959).

Weightman, J. G. "Alain Robbe-Grillet," *Encounter*, Vol. 18, No. 3 (March, 1962).

[47]

Weightman, J. G. The Novelist as Philosopher. New York, Oxford
University Press, 1962.
Weiner, Seymour S. "A Look at Techniques and Meaning in
Robbe-Grillet's *Le Voyeur*," *Modern Language Quarterly* (September, 1962).

EDITOR: William York Tindall
ADVISORY EDITORS
Jacques Barzun, W.T.H. Jackson
Joseph A. Mazzeo, Justin O'Brien

Distributed in the United Kingdom and Europe by
Columbia University Press, 440A, Hellfire Square, London E.C.4

COLUMBIA UNIVERSITY PRESS
New York and London